Managing Anger

90 Minute Guides

Michelle N. Halsey

Silver City Publications & Training, L.L.C.
P.O. Box 1914
Nampa, ID 83653
https://www.silvercitypublications.com/shop/

ISBN-10: 1-64004-004-8
ISBN-13: 978-1-64004-004-5

Contents

Chapter 1 – Anger Management

Anger can be an incredibly damaging force, costing people their jobs, personal relationships, and even their lives when it gets out of hand. However, since everyone experiences anger, it is important to have constructive approaches to manage it effectively.

Anger Management Review

Think of a situation where you experienced anger, preferably one that no longer affects you in the present time. Recall the exact symptoms you experienced, and the way you responded to the symptoms. The following guide questions can help during this process:

During your anger incident:

1. What symptoms did you experience

A. Physically?

B. Mentally?

C. Emotionally?

D. Behaviorally?

2. What was your response to your anger symptoms?

3. Was your response helpful? If yes, in what way was it helpful? If your response was not helpful, in what way was it unhelpful?

Chapter 2 – Understand Anger

Before we discuss specific anger management strategies, it is helpful to first understand the nature of anger. While most are familiar with this emotion, not everyone is aware of its underlying dynamics. In this module, we will discuss the cycle of anger, the fight or flight response, and common myths about anger.

The Cycle of Anger

Anger is a natural emotion that usually stems from perceived threat or loss. It's a pervasive emotion; it affects our body, thoughts, feelings, and behavior. Anger is often described in terms of its intensity, frequency, duration, threshold, and expression.

Anger typically follows a predictable pattern: a cycle. Understanding the cycle of anger can help us understand our own anger reactions, and those of others. It can also help us in considering the most appropriate response.

Illustrated below are the five phases of the anger cycle: **trigger, escalation, crisis, recovery, and depression.**

Phase 1: The Trigger Phase

The trigger phase happens when we perceive a threat or loss, and our body prepares to respond. In this phase, there is a subtle change from an individual's normal/ adaptive state into his stressed state. Anger triggers differ from person to person, and can come from both the environment or from our thought processes.

Phase 2: The Escalation Phase

In the escalation phase, there is the progressive appearance of the anger response. In this phase, our body prepares for a crisis after perceiving the trigger. This preparation is mostly physical, and is manifested through symptoms like rapid breathing, increased heart rate, and raised blood pressure. Once the escalation phase is reached there is less chance of calming down, as this is the phase where the body prepares for fight or flight (to be discussed later).

Phase 3: The Crisis Phase

As previously mentioned, the escalation phase is progressive, and it is in the crisis phase that the anger reaction reaches its peak. In the crisis phase our body is on full alert, prepared to take action in response to the trigger. During this phase, logic and rationality may be limited, if not impaired because the anger instinct takes over. In extreme cases, the crisis phase means that a person may be a serious danger to himself or to other people.

Phase 4: The Recovery Phase

The recovery phase happens when the anger has been spent, or at least controlled, and there is now a steady return to a person's normal/ adaptive state. In this stage, reasoning and awareness of one's self returns. If the right intervention is applied, the return to normalcy progresses smoothly. However, an inappropriate intervention can re-ignite the anger and serve as a new trigger.

Phase 5: The Depression Phase

The depression phase marks a return to a person's normal/ adaptive ways. Physically, this stage marks below normal vital signs, such as heart rate, so that the body can recover equilibrium. A person's full use of his faculties return at this point, and the new awareness helps a person assess what just occurred. Consequently, this stage may be marked by embarrassment, guilt, regret, and or depression.

After the depression phase is a return to a normal or adaptive phase. A new trigger, however, can start the entire cycle all over again.

Below is an example of a person going through the five stages of the anger cycle.

Josephine came home from work to see dirty plates left in the sink (trigger phase). She started to wash them, but as she was doing so she kept thinking about how inconsiderate her children are for not cleaning after themselves. She was already tired from work and does not need the extra chore. She felt the heat in her neck and the tremble in her hands as she's washing the dishes (escalation phase).

Feeling like she can't keep it to herself any longer, she stormed up the room to confront her kids. In a raised voice, she asked them how difficult could it be to wash the dishes. She told them that they are getting punished for their lack of responsibility (crisis phase).

Having gotten the words out, she felt calmer, and her heartbeat slowly returned to normal. She saw that her kids are busy with homework when she had interrupted them. She was also better able to hear their reasoning, as they apologized (recovery phase).

Josephine regretted yelling at her children and told them that she's simply tired and it's not their fault (depression phase).

NOTE: How long each phase lasts differ from person to person. Some people also skip certain phases, or else they go through them privately and/ or unconsciously.

Understanding Fight or Flight

The Fight or Flight theory, formulated by Walter Cannon, describes how people react to perceived threat. Basically, when faced with something that can harm us, we either aggress (fight) or withdraw (flight). It is believed that this reaction is an ingrained instinct geared towards survival.

The fight or flight instinct is manifested in bodily ways. When faced with a threat, our body releases the hormones adrenaline, noradrenaline, and cortisol. These chemicals are designed to take us to a state of alertness and action. They result in increased energy, heart rate, slowed digestion, and above normal strength.

Understanding the fight or flight instinct can help us understand the dynamics of our anger response. The following are some of the implications of the fight and flight theory on anger management:

First, the theory underscores how anger is but a natural response. There is no morality to anger. Anger is a result of perceived harm to self, whether physical or emotional.

Second, this theory reminds us of the need to stay in control. When we are angry, our rational self gets overridden by a basic survival instinct. There's a need to act immediately. This instinct can then result in aggressiveness, over-reactivity, and hyper-vigilance, which are all contrary to rational and deliberate response. Conscious effort towards self-awareness and control is needed so that this instinct does not overpower us.

Common Myths about Anger

Here are five common myths about anger:

Myth 1: Anger is a bad emotion.

There is no such thing as a good or bad emotion; they are instinctual reactions and we don't make conscious decisions for them to come. In fact, some anger reactions are appropriate, such as the anger against discrimination, injustice, and abuse. What can be judged as positive or negative/ healthy or unhealthy is how we react to anger.

Myth 2: Anger needs to be 'unleashed' for it to go away.

It's true that anger needs to be expressed in order for symptoms to be relieved. However, expressing anger in verbally or physically aggressive ways are not the only way to 'unleash' anger. Nor is anger an excuse for a person to be aggressive. The expression of anger can be tempered by rationality and forethought.

Note that venting anger does not necessarily results into the anger disappearing, although venting can relieve the symptoms. At times, processing personal experiences, seeing concrete change and genuine forgiveness are needed for anger to go away.

Myth 3: Ignoring anger will make it go away.

Generally, all kinds of emotions do not disappear when ignored. The anger just gets temporarily shelved, and will likely find other ways of getting expressed. It can get projected to another person, transformed into a physical symptom, or built up for a bigger future blow up.

Some of our behaviors may even be unconscious ways of expressing anger.

While there are situations when it's inadvisable to express your anger immediately, the very least you can do is acknowledge that it exists.

Myth 4: You can't control your anger.

This myth is related to the second one. As discussed earlier, the fight and flight instinct can make anger an overwhelming emotion. However, this instinct does not mean that you're but a slave to your impulses. Awareness of anger dynamics and a conscious effort to rise above your anger can help you regain control of your reactions.

Myth 5: If I don't get angry, people will think I am a pushover.

It's true that a person can lose credibility is he makes rules and then ignores violations. However, anger is not the only way a person can show that there are consequences to violations. In fact, the most effective way of instilling discipline in others is to have a calm, non-emotional approach to dealing with rule-breakers. Calm and rationality can communicate strength too.
Do's and Don'ts

Now that we've established that anger is a natural, unavoidable, and instinctual reaction, let's look at how we can respond to anger appropriately. In this module, we will discuss the dos and don'ts in responding to anger.

Unhelpful Ways of Dealing with Anger
The following are unhelpful ways of dealing with anger:

DON'T ignore the anger.

Some people respond to anger by not admitting, even to themselves, that they are angry. Defense mechanisms often used to ignore anger include laughing an issue off, distracting one's self from the problem, and trivializing the trigger's impact.

DON'T keep the anger inside.

There are people who do recognize that they're angry. However, they choose to obsess about their anger in silence rather than express it. They can bear grudges for a long time. People like this, also called 'stuffers', are more likely to develop hypertension compared to others. They are also likely to just 'explode' one day, once the anger has built to the point that they can't keep it inside anymore.

DON'T get aggressive.

The right to vent your anger doesn't extend to doing it in ways that can hurt others, hurt yourself, and damage property. Aggression can be verbal or physical.

DON'T get passive-aggressive.

Passive-aggressiveness refers to indirect and underhanded means to get back at the person who made you angry. Examples of passive-aggressive behaviors are gossiping, tardiness and backbiting.

DON'T use non-constructive communication styles.
Avoid the use of indirect attacks and unproductive statements. These include blaming, labeling, preaching, moralizing, ordering, warning, interrogating, ridiculing and lecturing.

Helpful Ways of Dealing with Anger
The following are helpful ways in dealing with anger:

DO acknowledge that you are angry.

It is important that you know how to recognize that you are angry, and give yourself permission to feel it. This can be as simple as saying to yourself "I am angry." Remember, you can't control something you don't admit exists!

DO calm yourself before you say anything.

In the previous discussions, we saw how there is a biological reason why anger can feel overwhelming --- our body is engaged in a fight or flight response. It helps then to defer any reactions until you have reached the return to normal/ adaptive phase of the anger cycle. Otherwise, you might end up saying or doing something that you'd later regret. Count 1 to 10!

DO speak up, when something is important to you.

This is the opposite to 'keeping it all in.' If a matter is important to you, so much so that keeping silent would just result in physical and mental symptoms, then let it out. If it's not possible to speak to the person concerned, at least look for a trusted friend or a mental health professional.

DO explain how you're feeling in a manner that shows ownership and responsibility for your anger.

Take ownership and responsibility for your feelings. This makes the anger within your control (you can't control other people). One way to take ownership and responsibility for your anger is through the use of I-messages, which would be discussed in a later module.

Gaining Control

Anger is instinctual, yes. It is an emotion that comes unbidden and we often don't have a choice whether we would be angry or not. What we can do however, is take control of our anger when it comes. In this module, we will discuss ways to gain control over our anger. Specifically we will discuss recognizing warning signs, coping thoughts, relaxation techniques and ways to blow off steam.

A Word of Warning

The first step in gaining control of anger is to recognize its warning signs. You have to be aware of symptoms that your anger is about to build up, so that you can catch yourself early and make the necessary intervention. This process involves taking yourself from the 'moment' and observing your own reactions from a third person point of view.

Warning signs of anger exists in a range. Some are very obvious; others very subtle. They differ from person to person.

Signs of anger can be physical, mental, emotional, and behavioral.

Physical signs of anger include:
- rapid heart rate
- difficulty breathing
- headache
- stomachache
- sweating
- feeling hot in the face and neck
- shaking

Mental signs of anger include:
- difficulty concentrating
- obsessing on the situation
- thinking vengeful thoughts
- cynicism

Emotional signs of anger include:
- sadness
- irritability
- guilt
- resentment
- feeling like you need to hurt someone
- needing to be alone
- needing to isolate one's self
- numbness

Behavioral signs of anger include:
- clenching of fist
- pounding of fist on a wall/ table or any surface
- pacing
- raising one's voice
- any act of aggression/ passive-aggression

Using Coping Thoughts

Once you realize that you are angry, or that you're about to get angry, you can start calming yourself mentally. The following are just a few mental scripts you can use to keep your anger under control.

1. Calm down first, and think this through.

2. This may not be as bad as it seems.

3. This is just one incident --- it doesn't define my life.

4. I am capable of managing this situation.

5. It's alright to be upset. / I have the right to be upset in this situation. / I am angry.

6. What needs to be done immediately? (damage control/ solution-focused mode).

7. Bad things/ Mistakes do happen/ Nothings says that things will go right all the time.

8. There is no need to feel threatened here.

9. I have no control over other people and their feelings. But I have control over myself.

10. I have managed anger successfully before and I will again.

Using Relaxation Techniques

Another way to help you control your anger is to intentionally induce yourself to a state of calm. This can help especially in addressing the physical symptoms of anger.

Relaxation techniques that you can do include:

Breathing Exercises

Deliberately controlling your breathing can help a person calm down. Ways to do this include: breathing through one's nose and exhaling through one's mouth, breathing from one's diagram, and breathing rhythmically.

Meditation

Meditation is a way of exercising mental discipline. Most meditation techniques involve increasing self-awareness, monitoring thoughts, and focusing. Meditation techniques include prayer, the repetition of a mantra, and relaxing movement or postures.

Progressive Muscle Relaxation (PMR)

PMR is a technique of stress management that involves mentally inducing your muscles to tense and relax. PMR usually focuses on areas of the body where tension is commonly felt, such as the head, shoulders, and chest area. It's a way to exercise the power of the mind over the body.

Visualization

Visualization is the use of mental imagery to induce relaxation. Some visualization exercise involves picturing a place of serenity and comfort, such as a beach or a garden. Other visualization exercises involve imagining the release of anger in a metaphorical form. An example of this latter kind of visualization is imagining one's anger as a ball to be released to space.

Music

Some people find listening to music as very relaxing. The kind of music that's calming differs from person to person; traditional relaxation music includes classical pieces, acoustic sounds, and even ambient noises.

Art and Crafts

There are people who find working with their hands as a good way to relax. This is especially true for people who feel their tensions in their hands. Drawing pictures, paper construction and sculpting are just some of the ways to de-stress when faced with an anger trigger. Arts and crafts are helpful because it keeps a person from obsessing on the anger while he or she is still in the recovery phase of the anger cycle.

Blowing Off Some Steam

Another way of controlling your anger is by getting the anger energy out--- blowing off steam. These techniques are especially helpful when you are in the crisis phase of the anger cycle.

The following are some constructive ways of blowing off steam:

Screaming

If the place would allow it, screaming can help release the tensions and frustrations that come with anger. Think of the thing that angers you the most, build momentum, and let it out in one big shout. You may also scream out the words you wish you could say if the venue is appropriate; the louder the scream, the better.

Physical Activity

Many people find exercise, sports, dancing and even just pacing about, as effective ways to vent anger. This makes sense; if the fight and flight response gears a person for physical action, then physical action might indeed be the best way to deal with the anger. Physical activity is also believed to release endorphins, our natural mood regulators.

Pillow Punching

The need to fight back may be channeled through punching pillows. Pillows provide a safe way to release tensions; it's safe not just for the object of the anger but also for one's self. Related techniques include wringing out towels and breaking old plates.

Writing

If physical activities are not your thing, you can blow off steam by expressing your thoughts and feelings in writing. You can write in an unstructured way, simply putting on paper the first thing that comes to your mind. You can also be more creative about it, and channel your anger through poetry or song.

Singing

Here's a new one: vent your anger by going to your nearest videoke or karaoke bar. Many people find singing therapeutic, especially if the song lyrics and melody matches one's mood.

Separate the People from the Problem

Anger is not just personal. It can be relational as well. When managing anger that involves other people, it helps to have a problem-oriented disposition, setting personal matters aside. This way the issue becomes an objective and workable issue.

In this module, we will discuss ways to separate people from the problem. Specifically, we will discuss the difference between objective and subjective language, ways to identify the problem, and how to use I-messages.

Chapter 3 – Objective versus Subjective Language

One way to make sure that a discussion remains constructive is to use objective rather than subjective language.

Objective language involves stating your position using reference points that are observable, factual, and free from personal prejudices. Objective references do not change from person to person.

This is the opposite of subjective language, which is vague, biased, and or emotional. You are using subjective language when you are stating an opinion, assumption, belief, judgment, or rumor.

The use of objective language keeps the discussion on neutral ground. It's less threatening to a person's self-esteem and therefore keeps people from being in the defensive. More importantly, objective language can be disputed and confirmed, which ensures that the discussion can go towards a solution.

Objective vs Subjective Language Guidelines

Here are some guidelines in the use of objective vs. subjective language:

State behaviors instead of personality traits.

Subjective: You're an *inconsiderate* supervisor.

Objective: You approved the rule without consulting with us first.

Avoid vague references to frequency. Instead, use the actual numbers.

Subjective: You are *always* late!

Objective: You were late for meetings four times in the past month.

Clarify terms that can mean differently to different people.

Subjective: You practice *favoritism* when you give promotions.

Objective: The employee ranking system is not being followed during promotions.

Don't presume another person's thoughts, feelings, and intentions.

Subjective: You hate me!

Objective: You do not talk to me when we are in a room together.

Don't presume an action you did not see or hear.

Subjective: She stole my wallet.

Objective: The wallet was in my desk when I left. It was no longer there when I came back, and she was the only person who entered the room.

Identifying the Problem

You can't separate people from the problem if you don't know what the problem is. A good way to move forward, in a discussion where anger is escalating, is through identifying the problem.

Identifying the problem focuses all energy on the crisis at hand rather than the persons involved in a conflict. The two parties focus their energies on a common enemy that is outside of themselves, a move that puts the two opposing parties back in neutral ground.

There are many processes you can use to identify the problem. Here is one of them:

STEP ONE: Get as much information as you can why the other party is upset.

STEP TWO: Surface the other person's position. Reframe this position into a problem statement. Example: *"I can hear how upset you are. Am I right in perceiving that the problem for you is that you weren't informed of the account being sold?"*

STEP THREE: Review your own position. State your position in a problem statement as well. Example: *"The problem for me is that I don't have the resources to contact you. The phone lines are not working because of the storm."*

STEP FOUR: Having heard both positions, define the problem in a mutually acceptable way. Example: *"I hear that you'd like to be informed of any sales. On my part, I'd like to inform you, but for as* long as the phone lines are dead, I can't see how I would do it. I think the issue here is about finding an alternative way to get the information to you on time while the phones are being repaired. Do you agree?"

If the two parties agree to the problem statement, they can now both work at the surfaced problem and take the focus away from their emotions.

Using "I" Messages

An "I-message" is a message that is focused on the speaker. When you use I-messages, you take responsibility for your own feelings instead of accusing the other person of making you feel a certain way. The opposite of an I-message is a You-message.

An "I-message" is composed of the following:

A description of the problem or issue.

Describe the person's behavior you are reacting to in an objective, non-blameful, and non-judgmental manner.

"When ... "

Its effect on you or the organization.

Describe the concrete or tangible effects of that behavior.

"The effects are ... "

A suggestion for alternative behavior.

"I'd prefer ... "

Here is an example of an I-message:

"When I have to wait outside the office an extra hour because you didn't inform me that you'd be late (problem/issue), I become agitated (effect). I prefer for you to send me a message if you will not be able to make it (alternative behavior)."

The most important feature of I-messages is that they are neutral. There is no effort to threaten, argue, or blame in these statements. You avoid making the other person defensive, as the essence of an I-message is "I have a problem" instead of "You have a problem". The speaker simply makes statements and takes full responsibility for his/her feelings.

Working on the Problem

The escalation of anger in 'hot' situations can be easily prevented, if a system for discussing contentious issues is in place. In this module, we will discuss how to work effectively on the problem. Specifically, we will tackle constructive disagreement, negotiation tips, building a consensus and identifying solutions.

Using Constructive Disagreement

There is nothing wrong with disagreement. No two people are completely similar therefore it's inevitable that they would disagree on at least one issue. There's also nothing wrong in having a position and defending it.

To make the most of a disagreement, you have to keep it constructive. The following are some of the elements of a constructive disagreement:

- **Solution-focus.** The disagreement aims to find a workable compromise at the end of the discussion.

- **Mutual Respect.** Even if the two parties do not agree with one another, courtesy is always a priority.

- **Win-Win Solution.** Constructive disagreement is not geared towards getting the "one-up" on the other person. The premium is always on finding a solution that has benefits for both parties.

- **Reasonable Concessions.** More often than not, a win-win solution means you won't get your way completely. Some degree of sacrifice is necessary to meet the other person halfway. In constructive disagreement, parties are open to making reasonable concessions for the negotiation to move forward.

- **Learning-Focus.** Parties in constructive disagreement see conflicts as opportunities to get feedback on how well a system works, so that necessary changes can be made. They also see it as a challenge to be flexible and creative in coming up with solutions for everyone's gain.

Negotiation Tips

Negotiations are sometimes a necessary part of arriving at a solution. When two parties are in a disagreement, there has to be a process that would surfaces areas of bargaining. When a person is given the opportunity to present his side and argue for his or her interests, anger is less likely to escalate.

The following are some tips on negotiation during a conflict:

Note situational factors that can influence the negotiation process.

Context is an important element in the negotiation process. The location of the meeting, the physical arrangement of room, as well as the time the meeting is held can positively or negatively influence the participants' ability to listen and discern. For example, negotiations held in a noisy auditorium immediately after a stressful day can make participants irritable and less likely to compromise.

Prepare!

Before entering a negotiating table, make your research. Stack up on facts to back up your position, and anticipate the other party's position. Having the right information can make the negotiation process run faster and more efficiently.

Communicate clearly and effectively.

Make sure that you state your needs and interests in a way that is not open to misinterpretation. Speak in a calm and controlled manner. Present arguments without personalization. Remember, your position can only be appreciated if it's perceived accurately.

Focus on the process as well as the content.

It's important that you pay attention not just to the words you and the other party are saying, but also the manner the discussion is running. For example, was everyone able to speak their position adequately, or is there an individual who dominates the conversation? Are there implicit or explicit coercions happening? Does the other person's non-verbal behavior show openness and objectivity? All these things influence result, and you want to make sure that you have the most productive negotiation process that you can.

Keep an open-mind.

Lastly, enter a negotiation situation with an open mind. Be willing to listen and carefully consider what the other person has to say. Anticipate the possibility that you may have to change your beliefs and assumptions. Make concessions.

Building Consensus

Consensus means unanimous agreement on an area of contention. Arriving at a consensus is the ideal resolution of bargaining. If both parties can find a solution that is agreeable to both of them, then anger can be prevented or reduced.

The following are some tips on how to arrive at a consensus:

Focus on interests rather than positions.

Surface the underlying value that makes people take the position they do. For example, the interest behind a request for a salary increase may be financial security. If you can communicate to the other party that you acknowledge this need, and will only offer a position that takes financial security into consideration, then a consensus is more likely to happen.

Explore options together.

Consensus is more likely if both parties are actively involved in the solution-making process. This ensures that there is increased communication about each party's positions. It also ensures that resistances are addressed.

Increase sameness / reduce differentiation.

A consensus is more likely if you can emphasize all the things that you and the other party have in common, and minimize all the things that make you different. An increased empathy can make finding common interests easier. It may also reduce psychological barriers to compromising. An example of increasing sameness/ reducing differences is an employer and employee temporarily setting aside their position disparity and looking at the problem as two stakeholders in the same organization.

Chapter 4 – Identifying Solutions

Working on a problem involves the process of coming up with possible solutions. The following are some ways two parties in disagreement can identify solutions to their problem.

- **Brainstorm.** Brainstorming is the process of coming up with as many ideas as you can in the shortest time possible. It makes use of diversity of personalities in a group, so that one can come up with the widest range of fresh ideas. Quantity of ideas is more important than quality of ideas in the initial stage of brainstorming; you can filter out the bad ones later on with an in-depth review of their pros and cons.

- **Hypothesize.** Hypothesizing means coming up with 'what if' scenarios based on intelligent guesses. A solution can be made from imagining alternative set-ups, and studying these alternative set-ups against facts and known data.

- **Adopt a Model.** You may also look for a solution in the past. If a solution has worked before, perhaps it may work again. Find similar problems and study how it was handled. You don't have to follow a model to the letter; you are always free to tweak it to fit the nuances of the current problem.

- **Invent Options.** If there has been no precedence for a problem, it's time to exercise one's creativity and think of new options. A way to go about this is to list down each party's interests and come up proposed solutions that have benefits for each party.

- **Survey.** If the two parties can't come up with a solution between the two of them, maybe it's time to seek other people's point of view. Survey people with interest or background in the issue in contention. Find an expert is possible. Just remember though, at the end of the day the decision is still yours. Identify a solution based on facts, not on someone's opinion.

Solving the Problem

After a constructive discussion of the problem, as well as review of available options, it's now time to go about solving the problem.

Solving a problem lessens its 'threat' aspect, making less an anger trigger. In this module, we will discuss elements of solving the problem. Particularly, we would discuss choosing a solution, making a plan, and getting it done.

Choosing a Solution

You've already identified possible solutions to a problem. The next thing to do is how to narrow the list down to the best.

The following are some criteria you can use when choosing solutions.

- **Costs and benefits.** An ideal solution is one that has the least costs and most benefits.

- **Disagreeing parties' interests**. An ideal solution has factored in the impact on all parties concerned and has made adjustments accordingly.

- **Foresight**. An ideal solution doesn't have just short-term gains bit long term ones as well.

Obstacles. An ideal solution has anticipated all possible obstacles in its implementation and has made plans accordingly.

VALUES. An ideal solution is one that is consistent with the mission-vision of the organization and/ or its individual members.

Making a Plan

You've already picked a solution for your problem. Now it's time to create a plan for its implementation.

The following are some guidelines when making a plan.

Keep your goal(s) central to you plan.

Every solution has a goal. The goal is the specific and measurable change that you want to achieve by implementing your solution. When you make a plan, make sure that all the steps and processes you outline are moving towards this goal.

Break down your action plan into concrete steps.

A good plan is concrete instead of abstract, specific instead of generic. Think of the different steps that you need to do in order to get to your ultimate goal and plan along those milestones. Note the deliverable per milestone. Indicate the timeline for each milestone. Identify the people responsible for each task.

Note all the resources you would need.

There are two kinds of resources: human and material. Make a list of all human and material resources that you need to execute the action, and make sure that they are all available. If they are not available, add an extra action plan to procure them. You want to make sure that your plan is realistic given your resources.

Plan how the solution would be evaluated.

A good plan doesn't just include the steps to execute the program. It should also include mechanisms for monitoring progress and evaluating results. An evaluation plan ensures that needs for plan revision can be surfaced.

Getting it Done

An issue in contention will remain a hot issue unless the plan is implemented. It is only when concrete change can be observed that anger can be seriously addressed.

The following are some tips in implementing a solution.

Stick to your plan.

Note the what, where, when and, who of your plan and follow it to the letter. This will keep your end of the bargain explicit and easy to monitor and evaluate. Deviating from the plan can result to additional anger, especially if you deviated in areas important to the other party.

Monitor progress and results.

Keep track of whether or not your solution is accomplishing the goal. Make sure that you put everything on paper for ready reference later. Log down best practices, risks and obstacles encountered.

Reward and revise accordingly.

If the solution is working, note progress and affirm the success. This gives the two parties a sense of accomplishment. More so, the next time they have a conflict, it can serve as testament to their ability to solve a problem.

If the solution is not working, gather feedback. Surface the reason why the solution does not seem to be working. Make the necessary changes so that you can revise the plan as needed.

A Personal Plan

Anger is deeply personal. Effective anger management should take into consideration individual anger dynamics and tailor-fit interventions to them. In this module we will discuss what hot buttons are, how to identify your personal hot buttons, and how you can be benefitted by keeping a personal anger log.

Chapter 5 – Understanding Hot Buttons

Hot buttons are triggers that make us react with anger. They are not necessarily the real cause of our anger, but they can be the one that 'lights the fuse'. Triggers vary in the intensity of the anger reaction they can evoke; some can evoke uncontrollable rage while others merely mild irritation.

Hot buttons can be things that fall short of your expectations, block your goals, attack your self-esteem, violate your values, and/ or give you a feeling of loss or helplessness. A hot button is usually one that elicits an intense reaction in a person, or the one that frequently sparks anger.

These hot buttons can be:

- Something we **observe** (e.g. injustices happening to other people)

- Something we **think** (e.g. the thinking that we are always the target of a particular person's mockery)

- Something we **feel** (e.g. the feeling of being helpless)

- Something we **do** (e.g. rescuing someone in a jam even if they don't deserve our help)

- Any **combination** of the four

Identifying Your Hot Buttons

Hot buttons differ from person to person. Our personal histories influence what would make us angry. Some triggers are caused by conditioning, modeling, and unresolved issues.

A key to seeing if a hot button is the real cause of the anger, or just a trigger, is to see if your anger reaction is proportionate to what the situation calls for. If you're angrier than you should be, perhaps there is an underlying emotional issue that needs to be surfaced.

Awareness of your hot buttons is already winning half the battle against anger. If you know what can evoke your anger, you can watch out for them.

A Personal Anger Log

More often than not, anger reactions appear in patterns. This means that there is a predictable structure that the anger reactions follow. This pattern is unique to each individual.

Unfortunately, it is difficult to notice this pattern unless you take that third person point of view and study your anger reactions from a distance.

Here is where keeping a personal anger log would help. A personal anger log is a diary of anger reactions including symptoms, triggers and coping styles. It is a way of increasing awareness of anger patterns unique to the individual. With awareness, one can better identify ways to prevent and cope with anger when it comes.

Keeping a personal anger log is also a good way to blow off steam. You may treat is as a diary. Instead of a structured table, as the one that will be presented later, you can make an unstructured one to note your free floating ideas and feelings.

Here is a sample template for a personal anger log:

My Personal Anger Log for Week x							
Date / Time	Symptoms	Before the anger, these are what I was:				My response to the anger:	Effect of my anger response:
		Seeing	Thinking	Feeling	Doing		
		Insights:					

The Triple A Approach

Anger is exacerbated by a feeling of victimization and helplessness. It helps to know then that we always have at least three options when dealing with an anger-provoking situation: you can alter, avoid or accept.

Alter

You are not a victim of your situation; you always have the option of taking a deliberate and well-thought out response to an anger-provoking situation. Your options typically fall into three categories: alter, avoid, or accept.

Alter means that you initiate change. You can change things in your environment that are within your control. You can also initiate changes within yourself.

The following are ways that you can change to deal with anger more effectively.

Change non-productive habits.

If you know that you have a particular way of doing things that often result into an anger situation, perhaps it's time to break the pattern. For example, if you know that mediating a family quarrel while your mind is tired from work often leads to blow-ups, then re-schedule family meetings to times when you're more relaxed.

Respectfully ask others to change their behavior and be willing to do the same.

You can't control other people's thoughts, feelings, and behavior. You can, however, let them know that you'd appreciate a change. Waiting for lightning to strike people with habits that irritate you will never get you anywhere, perhaps proactive communication can.

Change the way you view a situation.

Sometimes, it's our interpretation of a situation that makes us angry, rather than the situation itself. What you can do is change your way of thinking. For example, irrational thoughts like "I have to be perfect at all times" usually result in anger directed at one's self when failures happen. Maybe if you start thinking "It's alright to fail now and then," things would get easier.

Change the way you react to a situation.

You can also deliberately change the way you respond. Anger usually begets anger; we raise our voice when someone raises their voice to us. But if you take a moment and find other ways to respond, then maybe you can manage your anger better.

Avoid

Avoid means steering clear of situations that can make you angry.

The following are 'avoid' ways that you can do to deal with anger more effectively.

Steer clear of people who make you upset.

Anger is often triggered by interactions with difficult people, or people who just 'rub you the wrong way.' If you know that a person is eliciting an intense anger reaction in you, and you feel that you can't control it, then perhaps it's best that you just take action to avoid this individual.

Steer clear of your 'hot buttons.'

One of the advantages of knowing your hot buttons is that it enables you to structure your day in such a way that avoids them. For example, if too many deadlines make you angry and stressed, then learn time management --- or don't take more projects than you can handle. Saying 'no' is a good avoid response.

Remove yourself from a stressful situation immediately.
Another avoid intervention is to immediately remove yourself from a situation that might escalate your anger. For example, if a peer provokes your anger, you don't have to stay around to listen to what he has to stay. You can opt to walk away and address the issue another day.

Accept

Unfortunately, there are some things that we cannot change nor avoid. In this case, we have to accept them. This is true in many things that involve unrecoverable losses, like an accident or financial collapse.

The following are examples of accept responses to dealing with anger:

Find learning.

When you have no choice but to accept a situation, make the most of it by distilling the lessons from the experience. This way you can recover control by making proactive changes to prevent the situation from happening again.

Seek higher purpose.

Finding meaning can help in managing anger. Interpreting a situation based on one's faith life, or personal philosophy, can lessen its threatening impact on the self. For instance, there are people who think that every negative experience is an opportunity, a call for change.

Vent to a friend.

If you can't do anything but accept a situation, at the very least find someone to share your experience with. Venting with a trusted friend or a mental health professional can help you integrate the experience better in your life. This can help you move on faster and more effectively.

Chapter 6 – Dealing with Angry People

It is not just our own anger that can get overwhelming. Another person's blow up can also trigger intense reactions in us, including shock, fear, and even reactive rage. In this module we will discuss how we can effective deal with angry people. Specifically we will talk about the Energy Curve, de-escalation techniques, and guidelines on when to back away and what to do.

Understanding the Energy Curve

One of the tricky things about handling another person's anger is reacting in a way that will not escalate the anger. This is where an understanding of the Energy Curve can help.

The Energy Curve shows the pattern commonly found in angry reactions. It shows how angry reactions progress in stages, and in each stage there are appropriate responses.

Below is an illustration of the Energy Curve:

Here are some key points to note about the Energy Curve:

RATIONAL BEHAVIOR. The baseline of the curve is rational behavior. This is the stage when a reasonable discussion about the cause of the anger can happen. Before an angry reaction, a person is said to be in that 'rational' frame of mind. However, once the angry reaction takes root, people go into a state of mind not conducive to reasoning. It is important then to get the person *back* to a rational frame of mind.

IMPLICATION: You cannot reason with a person during these times: when their anger is taking off, at the height of their anger/ rage and even at the point when they are cooling down! You'll just waste a perfectly good argument.

TAKE OFF. Angry reaction slowly builds momentum, and the point when the anger is gaining energy is called the 'take off' stage. The way anger builds in intensity differs from person to person. For example, some people start with hostile facial reactions, which progresses to shouting, and which progresses to hitting the table. Other people build up anger in less obvious ways, they start with keeping quiet and then progresses to physically withdrawing themselves from other people. The anger would continue to build energy until it reaches its peak.

IMPLICATION: Anger naturally builds energy during the take off phase. Arguing back at this point in fact, any conversation would just be futile. Don't react! Respond.

SLOW DOWN. In this stage is the most intense of the person's reaction. It is a turning point; the reaction stops gaining momentum and begins a steady decline.

COOL DOWN. Once the angry reaction has reached its height, it will start to subside. You can tell by observing the person's behavior --- often their voices go down to a level tone, they are not moving their hands as much and they seem to breathe easier. Unless provoked further, the person will run out of steam. However, if you start arguing to the person or agitating the person even during this stage, the reaction can take off once again.

IMPLICATION: Only when the angry reaction has slowed down can you introduce supportive behavior. Supportive behavior can be any statement that acknowledges the anger, example: "I can see that this is an upsetting experience for you."

BACK TO RATIONAL BEHAVIOR. Once the individual has returned to this stage, you can begin to start talking about the problem reasonably. You may even start problem solving at this point.

SUMMARY: When a person is angry, just let them vent! It's the fastest way to deal with the situation.

De-escalation Techniques

De-escalation techniques are skilled interventions designed to facilitate a person's cooling down process, reduce the possibility of getting verbally or physically hurt, and gain control of the situation.

The following are examples of de-escalation techniques:

Practice active listening.

MOST OF THE TIME, ALL AN ANGRY PERSON NEEDS IS AN OPPORTUNITY TO TELL SOMEONE HOW THEY FEEL, AND HAVE THEIR ANGER ACKNOWLEDGED. SEEING THAT YOU ARE GENUINELY LISTENING TO THEIR GRIEVANCE CAN HELP LESSEN THE INTENSITY OF THEIR ANGRY REACTION.

THE FOLLOWING ARE SOME HELPFUL COMPONENTS OF ACTIVE LISTENING:

Show non-verbally that you are listening: Make sure that your posture shows openness. Establish eye contact. Speak in a soft, well-modulated, non-threatening tone of voice.

Reflect: Re-state what you hear from the person. Example: "This is what I heard from you: You are mad because the package did not arrive on time." You can also mirror back their body language in a tentative but objective, non-judgmental fashion. Example: "I can see that you're really upset. You are clasping the desk very tightly."

Clarify: Help the person make sense of their garbled, confusing, and or illogical statements. "Could you help me explain to me a bit more about what happened in the cafeteria? What do you mean by 'he bullied you'?

Increase personal space: Anger can escalate if a person feels that he is being stifled. Make sure your body language is non-threatening. Create distance between you and the person.

Help the person recover a sense of control: Angry people may feel victimized by a situation, and may need to recover even a small sense of control. You can help do this by:

1. Giving them choices.
    Example: "Would you like to move to a different area and talk?"
2. Seeking their permission to speak.
    Example: May I tell what I think about what just happened?
3. Focusing on immediate solutions.

Example: "What do you think we can do today to help solve this issue?"

Orient them to immediacy: People temporarily loses track of their immediate surroundings at the height of getting overwhelmed. Orienting the person to the time, his location, and who he is with can help de-escalate a person. It helps a person feel less threatened if he knows where he is and how he got there. The goal also is to shift him from attending to his overwhelming feelings to recovering rationality.

Invite criticism: Ask the angry person to voice his or her criticism of yourself or the situation more fully. You might say something like, "Go ahead. Tell me everything that has you upset. Don't hold anything back. I want to hear all you have to say."

Agree if possible. If not, agree to disagree: There are cases when anger is triggered by a legitimate grievance. In these cases, it can help a person lose steam by hearing someone validate the presence of injustice. At the very least, agreeing that a person has a right to the opinion they have can help de-escalate anger.

Reiterate your support: Emphasize your willingness to help. Example: "Okay. I don't know how this thing could have happened, but you have my assurance that I'll stay with you until we figure it out."

Set limits: Tell the person that you are willing to listen, but you'd appreciate that the tones down the expression of his anger.

Example is: "I'm listening right now. I'd like to talk, but without the shouting. When you shout it is distracting, and if this issue is important to you, then I want to be able to concentrate without hearing you raise your voice. Can we start again? How did I upset you? "

When to Back Away and What to Do Next

Not all angry reactions can be effectively dealt with. Here are situations when it is more advisable to back away:

When you are too affected by an issue to view it objectively.

De-escalating anger requires that you can take yourself out of an issue, even temporarily, and look at it objectively. However, if the issue has personal meaning for us, or we are too tired to properly intervene, then we don't have the resources to de-escalate the anger.

WHAT TO DO: Withdraw from the situation and talk to someone you trust about your own feelings.

When there are warning signs for verbal and/ or physical violence.

Your priority is always your well-being and safety.

Warning signs for violence include a history of violent behavior, severe rage for seemingly minor reasons, possession of weapons and threats of violence.

WHAT TO DO: Get as far away from the person as you can! Go to a public place.

When there is influence of mood-altering substances.

No de-escalating technique can help you deal with a person who has taken alcohol and mood-altering drugs (both legal e.g. some anti-depressants, and illegal e.g. hallucinogens).

WHAT TO DO: Disengage from the conversation and talk to them when they're sober!

When no amount of rational intervention seems to work.

There are moments when a person is hell-bent on raging, and the anger will escalate regardless of what intervention you use. It is possible that the strength of the anger is significantly more than the person's resources to cope. This is signaled by a tendency for the anger to still take off even after slowing down and cooling down, despite the absence of provocation.

WHAT TO DO: Disengage from the conversation and re-schedule the talk for another time.

When there are signs of serious mental health conditions.

While there are no categories of anger disorders in the Diagnostic Manual of Mental Disorders-IV (the reference of most mental health professionals), some serious mental health conditions are related to anger. In these cases, intensive therapy and/or psychiatric medications may be most appropriate. As a rule, people who suffer impairment of reality testing cannot be expected to be rational or reasonable.

Signs to watch out for: persecutory or paranoid delusions, hallucinations, past history of violence based on delusions.

Chronic and *rigid* patterns of the use of anger as coping mechanism may point to a personality disorder.

WHAT TO DO: Compassionate understanding is key! However, disengage yourself immediately as some psychotic symptoms are correlated with a tendency towards violence. Refer to the appropriate mental health professional.

Chapter 7 – Putting it All Together

We've now come to the conclusion of our workshop. So far, we've presented to you different techniques that can help you manage your anger better. In this module, we will show how these different techniques come together. We will also give additional tips to help you in practicing these anger management techniques more effectively.

Process Overview

The following diagram is a summary of all the anger management techniques discussed in this workshop. The techniques can be summarized into four main steps: be informed, be self-aware, take control, and take action.

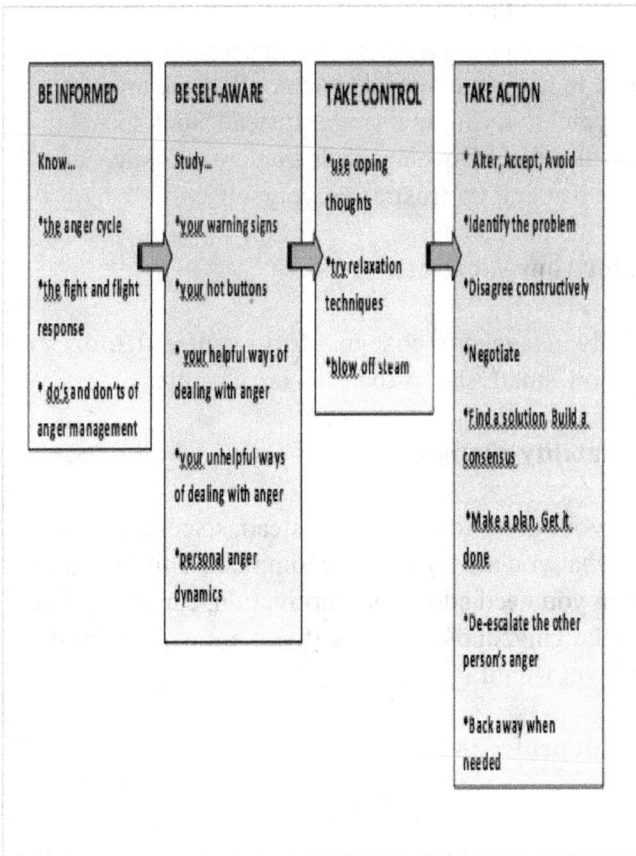

BE INFORMED	BE SELF-AWARE	TAKE CONTROL	TAKE ACTION
Know...	Study...	*use coping thoughts	* Alter, Accept, Avoid
*the anger cycle	*your warning signs	*try relaxation techniques	*identify the problem
*the fight and flight response	*your hot buttons	*blow off steam	*Disagree constructively
* do's and don'ts of anger management	* your helpful ways of dealing with anger		*Negotiate
	*your unhelpful ways of dealing with anger		*find a solution. Build a consensus.
	*personal anger dynamics		*Make a plan. Get it done
			*De-escalate the other person's anger
			*Back away when needed

Putting It into Action

The following are tips in putting anger management techniques into action:

Find your motivation

As with any plan towards behavioral change, it helps to sustain your motivation. Habits are hard to break and unless there is something strong that can inspire you to change, your efforts may not get followed through. So find your motivation! You can remember a negative effect of anger in your life, such as health problems or poor quality of relationships, and use it to encourage. You may also picture how things could be different if you can manage your anger better.

Choose only one change at a time.

Don't expect change to happen overnight. After all, these may be lifetime habits that you are trying to change. Instead, stick to managing one issue at a time. Develop goals that are realistic, otherwise you might just end up frustrating yourself.

Reward yourself for your successes.

If you've successfully managed to change, affirm yourself! Any success, no matter how small, shows that you are capable.

Choose an accountability partner.

It helps to not keep your goals to yourself. Instead, select a trusted friend who knows what you are trying to accomplish. This friend can encourage you when you need additional motivation, can spur you to action when you're lagging, and can check if you are working at the pace you promised you would.

Seek a mental health professional.

If you're really struggling with anger problems, or you just need additional support, remember: you can always seek a mental health professional. Counselors, therapists, and psychiatrist are all trained to address anger and its impact on your life.

Additional Titles

The 90 Minute Guide series of books covers a variety of general business skills and are intended to be completed in 90 minutes or less. It is an effective way for building your skill set and can be used to acquire professional development units needed by project managers and other industries to maintain their certification. For the availability of titles please see

www.silvercitypublications.com/shop/.

No. 1 - Appreciative Inquiry

No. 2 - Assertiveness and Self Control

No. 3 - Attention Management

No. 4 - Body Language Basics

No. 5 - Business Acumen

No. 6 - Business and Etiquette

No. 7 - Change Management

No. 8 - Coaching and Mentoring

No. 9 - Communications Strategies

No. 10 - Conflict Resolution

No. 11 - Creative Problem Solving

No. 12 - Delivering Constructive Criticism

No. 13 - Developing Creativity

No. 14 - Developing Emotional Intelligence

No. 15 - Developing Interpersonal Skills

No. 16 - Developing Social Intelligence

No. 17 - Employee Motivation

No. 18 - Facilitation Skills

No. 19 - Goal Setting and Getting Things Done

No. 20 - Knowledge Management Fundamentals

No. 21 - Leadership and Influence

No. 22 - Lean Process and Six Sigma Basics

No. 23 - Managing Anger

No. 24 - Meeting Management

No. 25 - Negotiation Skills

No. 26 - Networking Inside a Company

No. 27 - Networking Outside a Company

No. 28 - Office Politics for Managers

No. 29 - Organizational Skills

No. 30 - Performance Management

No. 31 - Presentation Skills

No. 32 - Public Speaking

No. 33 - Servant Leadership